Hong Kong Trail

Prior to the founding of Hong Kong as a British colony in 1841, the largest settlements on Hong Kong Island were fishing villages at Aberdeen and Stanley. The new Victorian administrators set about creating a modern city from scratch: reclaiming land, building dockyards, godowns and grand public buildings, introducing electricity, sanitation and telegraphs, and laying out roads and tramways. All this was good for business. Chinese and Europeans arrived by the boatload, turning the fledgling port into a prosperous trading hub.

Commerce was focused on the harbour, and the south side of the island remained remote until the 1920s. The cool heights of The Peak were developed as a retreat for colonial taipans, and a road was eventually extended around the coast to Repulse Bay, where a genteel hotel was built. Shek O was likewise endowed with a golf course and members' club.

But a reversal of fortunes was near. Hong Kong Island became a major battleground in 1941, when Commonwealth forces fought a losing defence against Japanese attackers. For the next four years, the territory lived under occupation. Wartime relics – bunkers, field kitchens and gun emplacements – can still be found crumbling amid the greenery. After the war, Hong Kong regained its footing, and huge inflows of refugees from China during the 1950s, 60s and 70s provided the labour and know-how to fuel a new economic miracle.

The British had forested the bare hillsides and built reservoirs high in the mountains to supply water to the city. These protected catchment zones would later become the heart of the country parks which today provide a back garden for urban residents. The Hong Kong Trail follows a 50 km route through these parks, allowing views of cityscape and coast from above. Whichever stage you walk, you'll find startling conjunctions of city and country, new and old, busy and remote – tangible signs of the contradictions which embody Hong Kong itself.

Concrete Plans for our Threatened Country Parks

When it comes to the priceless treasures that make up our magnificent country parks, sustained encroachment is slowly but surely eroding a resource that is unique among the densely populated cities of China. Gratuitous development nibbling at the fringes of our beautiful coastlines, mountains and valleys, should concern hikers specifically but also all who care about Hong Kong's heritage.

We would do well to beware of government-speak such as 'beautification' and 'improvement' when we hear of plans to make the landscape more attractive. **The natural world is already beautiful. Government cement will not make it more so.** The often mindless waste of taxpayers' money is cruelly obvious on many trails: the authorities have flattened undulating paths with bare concrete, channelled once-vibrant streams into square-sided concrete drains, and on even gentle climbs has built uninspiring concrete steps and bomb-proof railings of heavy-duty steel, destroying our children's natural heritage.

The damage done by the authorities is an affront to the hiker who enjoys the sensation of the earth, the crunch of gravel, leaves, roots and pebbles underfoot, and the exhilaration of a challenging climb. One is unlikely to venture outdoors looking forward to countless concrete-cast steps and a hard, heat-glaring cement surface to hike along.

Our meddling mandarins have little idea about the world of nature. We call upon the **Leisure & Cultural Services Department** to leave our country parks as nature intended; and perhaps spend the money saved on beautifying the urban areas instead.

FormAsia Books

In the annually compiled rankings of Asian cities, in which the likes of Shanghai and Singapore are regularly held up as pretenders to Hong Kong's position as first choice amongst expats, enlightened minds ought to pay more attention to the SAR's natural assets; for it's these which make the city so liveable, and in this respect its rivals don't come close.

For all its imperial treasures, Beijing has no precipitous peaks overhanging its city centre; Shanghai has a beautiful bund, but is somewhat deficient in the offshore island department; Bangkok is good for a lot of things, but instant access to deserted beaches is not one of them. Thanks to a quirk of Victorian land-leasing, Hong Kong combines the clamour of high-density city life with the restorative peace available only on high, windswept mountain ridges and green, undeveloped coastlines: a meeting of extremes which, allowing outdoor pursuits such as hiking, climbing and sailing, helps to preserve the health and sanity of many a foreign resident.

In this very visual guidebook, we lead you stage-by-stage along the four long-distance trails which have been marked out across Hong Kong Island and the New Territories. Your journey of a thousand miles is likely to start with a ride on the MTR rather than a single step, for all the routes described here are easily reached by public transport. Tackle each stage separately, or bring a tent and make a weekend of it and spend a night away from the usual neon glow, you may make the arresting discovery that there are indeed stars in the Hong Kong sky.

Compiling and photographing this book has been a major task, but one which has benefited everyone involved in it. We hope you will appreciate the variety of Hong Kong's rugged side as much as we do – and if you have discovered a different attraction or beaten a new path or for that matter found an error in this guide, we'd be pleased to hear from you at: needinfo@formasiabooks.com.

Hong Kong Trail

Few people in Hong Kong have gardens of their own. This rarely seems to matter, since we have the lush country parks of Hong Kong Island so close at hand. The more accessible parts are occupied at all times by joggers, dog lovers, morning walkers and

tai chi devotees. Other more remote sections can give you cause to wonder whether you are still in Hong Kong at all. The Hong Kong Trail opens up unusual places and striking vistas of the island you would otherwise be unlikely to see.

	Stage	Route
	Stage **1** **The Peak** 山頂	The Peak 山頂 > Pok Fu Lam Reservoir Road 薄扶林水塘道
	Stage **2** **Pok Fu Lam** 薄扶林	Pok Fu Lam Reservoir Road 薄扶林水塘道 > Peel Rise 貝璐道
	Stage **3** **Aberdeen** 香港仔	Peel Rise 貝璐道 > Wan Chai Gap 灣仔峽
	Stage **4** **Wong Chuk Hang** 黃竹坑	Wan Chai Gap 灣仔峽 > Wong Nei Chung Gap 黃泥涌峽
	Stage **5** **Jardine's Lookout** 渣甸山	Wong Nei Chung Gap 黃泥涌峽 > Mount Parker Road 柏架山道
	Stage **6** **Tai Tam** 大潭	Mount Parker Road 柏架山道 > Tai Tam Road 大潭道
	Stage **7** **Tai Tam Bay** 大潭灣	Tai Tam Road 大潭道 > To Tei Wan 土地灣
	Stage **8** **Tai Long Wan** 大浪灣	To Tei Wan 土地灣 > Tai Long Wan 大浪灣

Distance in km	Duration	Challenge
7.0	2.00	👢👢 *A fairly challenging walk*
4.5	1.50	👢👢 *A fairly challenging walk*
6.5	1.75	👢👢 *A fairly challenging walk*
7.5	2.00	👢 *Easy rambling*
4.0	1.50	👢👢👢 *Strenuous hiking*
4.5	1.50	👢 *Easy rambling*
7.5	2.00	👢 *Easy rambling*
8.5	2.75	👢👢👢 *Strenuous hiking*

total **50**

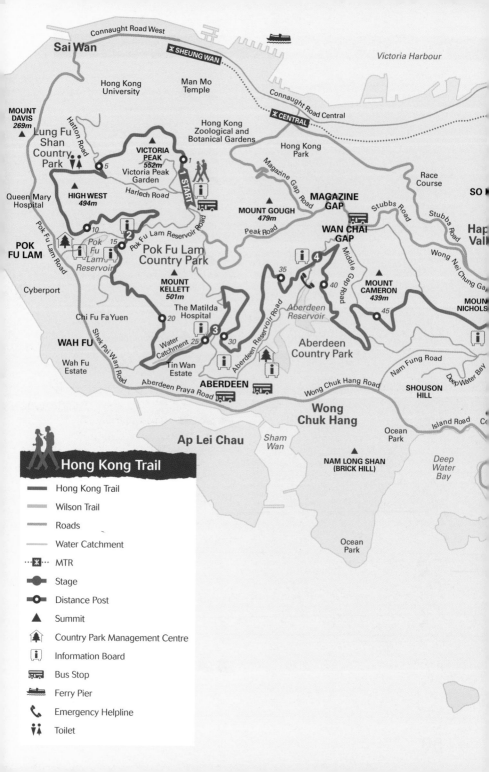

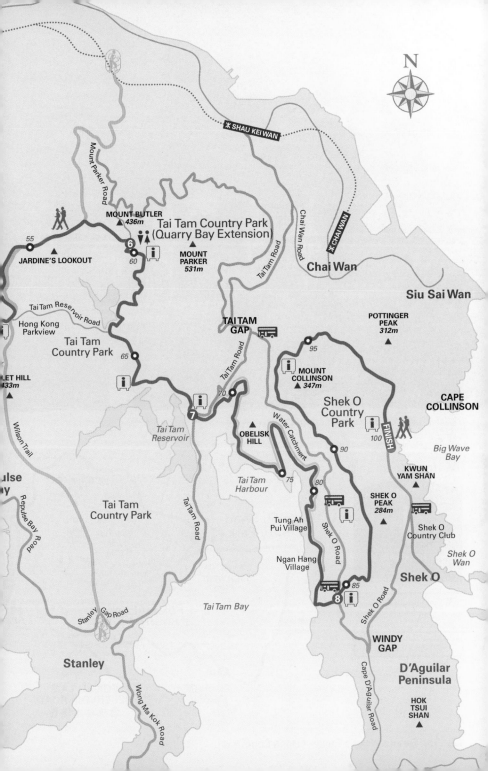

H003 Privileged panorama: Lugard's view

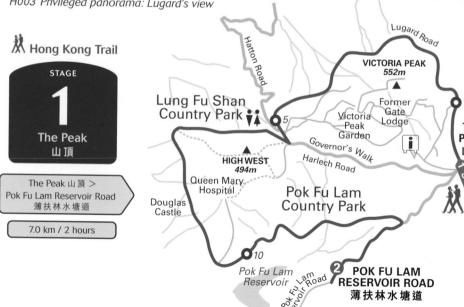

🚶 Hong Kong Trail

STAGE

1

The Peak
山頂

The Peak 山頂 >
Pok Fu Lam Reservoir Road
薄扶林水塘道

7.0 km / 2 hours

Lugard Road

VICTORIA PEAK
552m

Hatton Road

Lung Fu Shan
Country Park 🚻

5

Victoria
Peak
Garden

Former
Gate
Lodge

ℹ️

HIGH WEST
494m

Governor's Walk

Harlech Road

Queen Mary
Hospital

Pok Fu Lam
Country Park

Douglas
Castle

10

Pok Fu Lam
Reservoir

Pok Fu Lam
Reservoir Road

2 **POK FU LAM**
RESERVOIR ROAD
薄扶林水塘道

T
PI
L

1 St

> Starting at The Peak

Hop on the Peak Tram from Garden Road, bus 15 from Exchange Square or green minibus 1 from IFC to the Peak.

Pass the Peak Lookout, originally a rest pavilion for sedan chair bearers, to join Lugard Road on your right. The first low-rise colonial building serves as the headquarters for the Peak Tram manager. Keep an eye out for the statue of a deer behind the Peak Tower, placed there for feng shui purposes.

Lugard Road, named after Hong Kong's fourteenth governor, was built in the late 19th century on the lines of a hilltop resort, similar to the practice followed for senior administrators of other warm colonies. Elevation was

High and low: a privileged few get to live low-rise on the Peak

H008 Lamma Island – nirvana for the non-indigenous

regarded as more than a status symbol; it ensured altitudes more scenically commanding and less deleterious to physical wellbeing.

Native plants, including an impressive India Rubber Tree, were planted to give shade. Even today no traffic is allowed on what remains essentially a Victorian-era promenade, although several very upscale residences line the route – elaborate mailboxes giving a clue as to what lies concealed beyond ornamental gates.

As you wind your way around the northern slopes of Victoria Peak, spectacular views unfold below, first of the city and its harbour, framed by the Kowloon hills, and then of the western approaches, busy with shipping from all over the world. Further down the slope, another of Lugard's legacies – the University of Hong Kong – sprawls across the hillside above Sheung Wan.

The playground at the far end of Lugard Road, an open-air spot usually noisy with picnicking families, marks the confluence of four roads and at least two footpaths. An engraved stone commemorating the Middlesex Regiment used to stand here, but was spirited away to England prior to the handover ceremonies. Keeping the toilet block on your right, head down Harlech Road as it makes a gentle descent westwards. *H006* on the left-hand side confirms your route.

At *H007*, the road ends at a viewpoint on a spur of High West. Further down, the green slopes and terraced cemeteries of Pok Fu Lam descend to the Lamma Channel, where misty outlying islands intersect the shipping lanes. The lone hill directly ahead is Mount Davis, topped by powerful wartime gun emplacements. Bearing left now, the trail slopes downward a short distance before embarking on a forested section crossed by streams.

The crenellated Douglas Castle mansion

Shortly an open area is reached where one can enjoy views of calm Pok Fu Lam Reservoir directly below. In the distance you glimpse the battlement-roofed folly of Douglas Castle, a mansion built as steamship staff quarters in the nineteenth century and nowadays converted as a university hostel. The next stage of the Hong Kong Trail can be seen slicing through greenery far ahead, overlooked by expensive apartment blocks on the ridge of Mount Kellett. Steps lead down from here to the reservoir dam, but we turn left.

South of the island – sun dappled track

Keeping to a rough contour and heading back inland, the trail crosses half a dozen steep, rocky streams which are transformed into raging torrents during the rainy season. You may see green gauze netting tied

H009 Post haste

H013 Woodland haven

around the branches of shrubs; this is done by herbalists who will come back at a later stage to harvest the berries used in traditional medicine.

A bridge helps you over the unnamed stream which flows down from Victoria Gap. Soon after, the path joins the quiet Pok Fu Lam Reservoir Road, and here you must decide which way to return home: left and uphill at *H014*, heads for the Peak, while downhill lies Pok Fu Lam Road and buses to Central.

Velvet valley: Pok Fu Lam Reservoir and the Lamma Channel

Hong Kong Trail

STAGE
2
Pok Fu Lam
薄扶林

Pok Fu Lam Reservoir Road
薄扶林水塘道 >
Peel Rise 貝璐道

4.5 km / 1.5 hours

POK FU LAM RESERVOIR ROAD
薄扶林水塘道

Pok Fu Lam Reservoir Road

Pok Fu Lam Reservoir

Riding School

Ser Res

Hacking Trail

Chi Fu Fa Yuen

Wah Fu Estate

Ser Res

MOUNT KELLETT
501m

Matilda Hospital

Peel Rise

PEEL RISE
貝璐道

Water Catchment

Tin Wan Estate

ABERDEEN

Shek Pai Wan Road

15 20 25

Starting at Pok Fu Lam Reservoir Road

Either take public transport to the Peak and then follow the pedestrian Pok Fu Lam Reservoir Road downhill; or catch any bus from the Central Ferry Piers headed for Aberdeen, and hop off at the turning nearest the Pok Fu Lam Riding School, walking uphill past the reservoir.

The refreshing rush of streams after unexpected rains

Pokfulam, Hong Kong University Campus and the East Lamma Channel beyond

The start of Stage 2 is marked, if you're lucky, by a rare cluster of yellow wild orchids sprouting from a rock face turned silver by a constant trickle of water on your left. Follow the road downhill for a short distance to the fork and turn left – or right if coming from the riding school. Pass the service reservoir at *H015*, and turn sharp left again. You can't lose your way, which is very clearly signposted. Scale the steps on the left towards Peel Rise. At the junction bear left in the direction of Chi Fu – Peel Rise.

Passing through an area of tall grass and young trees, with occasional views out to sea, you soon join another paved road which, despite many forks, is linked to no other roads at all. You can be confident of meeting no cars as you hike, but you may encounter horses from the riding school further downhill.

Turn right at the junction. The road circles Mount Kellett, flanked by beautiful mature trees. Out to the west, the new Cyberport is visible on what was

formerly – and appropriately – named Telegraph Bay. Baguio Villas loom in the foreground, the vast dormitories of Wah Fu and Wah Kwai Estates lie further south, and behind their cubist monoliths floats Lamma Island.

Where the road peters out at the PCCW helpline, the Hong Kong Trail parts company by continuing straight ahead down a flight of steps, passing on its way a Chinese-style pavilion with upturned eaves. At *H022*, a sign points towards Peel Rise. The route heads eastwards now, alongside a rock-hewn catchwater, with Aberdeen below providing a scenic as well as noisy background. Known in Chinese as Little Hong Kong, it has always been busy with water traffic, and today is no different.

The catchwater and Stage 2 both end by the sandy riverbed at Peel Rise. If departing the trail at this juncture, follow the road downhill to Aberdeen and the bus station.

H022 Little Hong Kong: the prospering anchorage at Aberdeen

Aberdeen Harbour: yesterday's boat people now live in towers on land

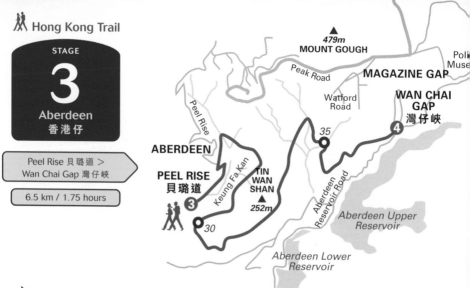

Hong Kong Trail

STAGE 3 Aberdeen 香港仔

Peel Rise 貝璐道 >
Wan Chai Gap 灣仔峽

6.5 km / 1.75 hours

> ## Starting at Aberdeen

Take any bus to the Aberdeen terminus and walk inland to the recently rebuilt Tin Hau Temple. Follow the road to the right of the temple. Turn left onto Peel Rise and walk uphill to reach Aberdeen Country Park, which marks the start of Stage 3.

Traffic-free Peel Rise climbs all the way to Peak Road, signposted near *H025*. The route initially follows this wide track before taking a right-hand turn to Wanchai Gap beyond the next marker and striking out into the tree-shaded valley of Keung Fa Kan, or Ginger Flower Brook. For the next hour or so, the hiker treads a soft carpet of fallen leaves, overhung by thick trees that provide welcome shade from the midday sun. At the junction near *H030*, follow the sign in the direction of the Aberdeen Reservoir Road.

A looping circuit of Tin Wan Shan delivers dark green views of the Aberdeen Reservoirs. The laughter of picnicking families and barbecue enthusiasts drifts up over the trees to reach your ears. Meandering north along a level contour, the trail passes escape routes to Watford Road (ten paces short of *H035*) and Aberdeen Reservoir Road, useful if you need to cut the hike short.

The surrounding vegetation is lush and obviously well-watered by the precipitous streams which cross the path at regular intervals. These idyllic hiking conditions, some of the best you'll experience anywhere in Hong Kong, prevail for more than five kilometres: from *H026* all the way through to *H037*.

The trail continues on an easy level to finish at Aberdeen Reservoir Road.

Buses for Central can be found by taking the road uphill past the garden and Police Museum (open until 5:00 pm, closed on Mondays and public holidays) to Wan Chai Gap.

Ideal hiking on natural terrain

H026 Rivulet of rocks

The Aberdeen reservoirs are enveloped in lush green forest

Authentic stone pathway – long may it remain

STAGE

4

Wong Chuk Hang
黃竹坑

Wan Chai Gap 灣仔峽 >
Wong Nei Chung Gap
黃泥涌峽

7.5 km / 2 hours

WAN CHAI GAP
灣仔峽

Middle Gap Road

Lady Clementi's Ride

40

Aberdeen Upper
Reservoir

MOUNT CAMERON
439m ▲

Black's Link

Aberdeen Tunnel

Aberdeen
Country Park

45

Wong Nei Chung
Gap Road

**MIDDLE
GAP**

**MOUNT
NICHOLSON**
430m ▲

Lady Clementi's Ride

WONG CHUK HANG

Water Catchment

Nam Fung Road

Deep Water Bay Road

50

**JARDINE'S
LOOKOUT**
• Petrol
Station

5

**WONG NEI
CHUNG GAP**
黃泥涌峽

Repulse Bay Road

Starting at Wan Chai Gap

Bus 15 from Exchange Square heads for the Peak. Alight at Wan Chai Gap by the end of Stubbs Road. Or, for a little additional exercise, start at the old Post Office on Queen's Road East and climb to the gap by following the steep Wan Chai Green Trail. Walk across to the small park, where the refreshment stand is usually ready with cold drinks, and take Aberdeen Reservoir Road downhill for a short distance to the beginning of Stage 4.

Reservoir resident

A world apart: the less-developed southern slopes of Hong Kong Island overlook Aberdeen Reservoir

H041 Perfect camouflage: wartime pillbox hidden by the years

The trail branches off to the left (or to the right, if continuing on from Stage 3) along Lady Clementi's Ride. The level track is named for the wife of Sir Cecil Clementi, a former Governor of Hong Kong (1925-30) who has his own eponymous Ride above Jardine's Lookout. Lady Clementi was a notorious prude. She vetted all the books bought for the Helena May Library. Any reference to a kiss or a cuddle and the book was out.

Her trail winds along the thickly forested valley above the reservoirs. Ruined pillboxes and gun emplacements, reminders of the Second World War, are partly lost in the undergrowth. Several, on the left-hand side, near *H041* are almost completely overgrown and are easy to miss.

Before reaching the dam of the upper reservoir, a left turn downhill is made for Black's Link via Middle Gap. The pleasing dirt trail keeps to a water catchment, with views over Wong Chuk Hang. At *H043* you bear left, traversing the catchment, onto a service road which snakes uphill. Then, at the fork between

H044 and *H045*, turn sharply right. The track rounds the southern slope of Mount Cameron, emerging onto Black's Link half an hour later.

This pedestrian road is named after Major-General W. Black, who was left in charge of the government for most of 1898. He demanded the construction of this road, linking Wong Nei Chung Gap with Magazine Gap ostensibly for defence purposes,

The delicate white Catherine wheel

but also because the army had purchased a hotel on the Peak to use as barracks. On both counts, the general made himself unpopular with the Peak's otherwise exclusively civilian residents.

Here we part company with the dirt path and turn right to carry on eastwards. Police signs affixed here and there warn dog owners to muzzle their mutts, since the infamous 'Mid-Levels Dog Poisoner' is still at large and active here as well as on Bowen Road. Near a mapboard, a rough scramble over giant boulders offers a detour up to the summit of Mount Nicholson.

H045 Aerial viewpoint

On its final stretch, Black's Link passes a collection of ostentatious palaces perched on ugly concrete stilts, allowing their inhabitants to overlook the island's southern coasts. The halfway stage *H050* is found here, though it is overshadowed by overpriced apartment blocks. Stage 4 ends conveniently near the bus stop on Deep Water Bay Road. Buses depart from here very frequently to various points in the city below.

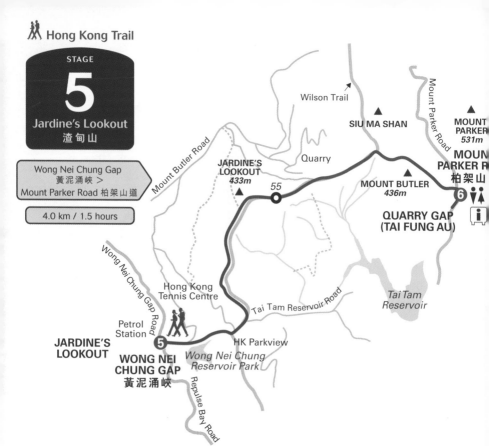

Hong Kong Trail

STAGE

5

Jardine's Lookout
渣甸山

Wong Nei Chung Gap
黃泥涌峽 >
Mount Parker Road 柏架山道

4.0 km / 1.5 hours

Wilson Trail

SIU MA SHAN

Quarry

JARDINE'S LOOKOUT *433m*

55

MOUNT BUTLER *436m*

MOUNT PARKER *531m*

MOUN PARKER R 柏架山

Mount Butler Road

Mount Parker Road

6

QUARRY GAP (TAI FUNG AU)

Tai Tam Reservoir

Hong Kong Tennis Centre

Tai Tam Reservoir Road

Petrol Station

JARDINE'S LOOKOUT

5

WONG NEI CHUNG GAP 黃泥涌峽

Wong Nei Chung Reservoir Park

HK Parkview

Wong Nei Chung Gap Road

Repulse Bay Road

> ## Starting at Wong Nei Chung Gap

Board either buses 6 or 66 at Exchange Square. Alight at the stop near the Cricket Club at Wong Nei Chung Gap. The name refers to the yellow muddy river which once flowed down through Happy Valley to the sea.

H051 Paddling beneath Parkview

Passing the petrol station, mount the flight of steps on the left to join Tai Tam Reservoir Road. The trail rises steadily, past the stone retaining walls of the Wong Nei Chung Reservoir near *H051*, to the vast residential complex of Parkview. A supermarket here allows you a last chance to stock up with drinks.

You can't miss the wooden archway which allows access to the Tai Tam Country Park. It may strike you as an overly triumphal gesture, quite disproportionate to the simple hiking trail it is there to introduce.

A gateway greeting for two major trails

The path joins forces here with the Wilson Trail, and together they head north to the summit of Jardine's Lookout. Here at *H052*, is erected a sombre black-marble memorial in honour of the Winnipeg Grenadiers – a reminder of Canada's contribution to the defence of Hong Kong during the Second World War. This promontory at *H055*, offers an amazing panorama (following spread) of the city and harbour, Wan Chai and Causeway Bay acting as foreground for the dramatic office towers of Central. The unusual angle of view clearly shows how close the city lies to the green mountains which encircle it.

H052 Staunch defenders from distant shores

H053 Pleasing perspective: south of the Island

H055 *Jardine's Lookout: a fresh perspective on the city below*

Kowloon laid bare for mid-week hikers

Moving on, the trail skirts the quarry at Mount Butler Road and bids farewell to the Wilson Trail near *H058*. We continue east in the general direction of Gulliver's giant golf ball, which sits teed up on Mount Parker as if ready to be struck across the water towards Kowloon. A slow ascent is now made to the pointed summit of Mount Butler, part of the way enclosed by high foliage, forming a corridor through verdant bamboo.

Great views of the varied Tai Tam reservoirs (following spread) are available from this vantage point, ranging from the Intermediate Reservoir with its impressively tall dam to traffic crossing the main spillway. A viewing compass helps you identify landmarks such as Redhill and Tai Tam Harbour.

Descend by way of no fewer than 589 steps to Quarry Gap (or in Chinese, Great Wind Pass), where there is an open picnic area in which to allow brief respite to sore ankles. To return to the city, take Mount Parker Road downhill to Quarry Bay – a rather long walk. Or continue straight on to Stage 6.

H056 Spot light on the steel forest: a citadel of commerce

First glimpse of the South

H057 Kai Tak panorama: looking across at Kowloon

Tai Tam Country Park, beloved green lung of the city

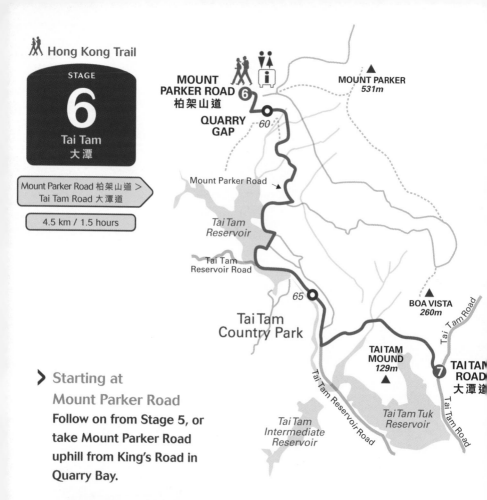

Hong Kong Trail

STAGE 6
Tai Tam 大潭

Mount Parker Road 柏架山道 >
Tai Tam Road 大潭道

4.5 km / 1.5 hours

MOUNT PARKER ROAD 柏架山道

QUARRY GAP

60

Mount Parker Road

MOUNT PARKER
531m

Tai Tam Reservoir

Tai Tam Reservoir Road

65

BOA VISTA
260m

Tai Tam Road

Tai Tam Country Park

TAI TAM MOUND
129m

7

TAI TAM ROAD 大潭道

Tai Tam Reservoir Road

Tai Tam Tuk Reservoir

Tai Tam Intermediate Reservoir

> **Starting at**
> **Mount Parker Road**
> **Follow on from Stage 5, or take Mount Parker Road uphill from King's Road in Quarry Bay.**

Leaf frog

The beginning of Stage 6 is a long way inside the country park boundaries. Reach it by following on from Stage 5, or by taking Mount Parker Road uphill from King's Road in Quarry Bay, passing the elegant colonial mansion of Woodside on your way. A funicular railway once made this ascent for the benefit of Swire staff, who kept holiday homes in the cooler climate of the pass; alas no longer!

Refreshing rush of reservoir rains

Bridge over calm waters

Splendid stonework: the Victorian-era Tai Tam reservoirs

Space, sun and solitude

The road downhill from Quarry Gap at *H060* is paved but free of traffic and well forested on either side. Birds twitter in hidden thickets. Emerging from the trees, the road reaches the highest Tai Tam Reservoir, and you cross its wedding-cake dam to the sound of gently lapping water at *H063*. Fishing in the various Tai Tam reservoirs is now permissible between the months of September to March. To apply for the $28 Fishing Licence, call the Water Supplies Department: 2824-5000 or apply: www.wsd.gov.hk.

Following the signs, you join the route of a road first laid in 1847, passing the beautiful granite walls of the lower dam and a neglected old milestone recording the distance between Victoria and Stanley. Then, further downhill beyond *H065* the trail makes a left turn and leaves the paved track to run a wilder course over rocks, ravines and river beds: fabulous hiking conditions which come to an end too soon. Skirting the red clay banks of the lowest reservoir, you soon arrive at Tai Tam Road and the edge of the country park at *H068*.

Bus 14 will take you to the MTR at Sai Wan Ho, or you can carefully cross the busy road and walk towards the narrow main dam for buses headed for Stanley.

Post-typhoon waters trapped in rock pools

Hong Kong Trail

STAGE
7
Tai Tam Bay
大潭灣

Tai Tam Road 大潭道 >
To Tei Wan 土地灣

7.5 km / 2 hours

OBELISK HILL
164m

Water Catchment

Shek O Road

7
TAI TAM ROAD
大潭道

Obelisk

75

Lan Nai Wan Village

Tai Tam Harbour

Lan Nai Wan

80

Tai Tam Road

Shek O Country Park

Tung Ah Village

Tung Au Pui Village

Ngan Hang Village

Red Hill Peninsula

Shek O Road

TO TEI WAN
土地灣

8

Nam Kee Café

To Tei Wan Village

> ## Starting at Tai Tam Road
> **Take the MTR to Sai Wan Ho and board Bus No.14. Alight at the stop immediately before the bus crosses the giant main dam, opposite the aquamarine-coloured waterworks building. Walk back, taking great care as there is no pavement, until you meet the olive-green railings on the right. Take the path downhill.**

Into the bush

Tai Tam Bay and the reservoir overpass

Weekend heroes take to the water

Lime-yellow temple at Lan Nai Wan   *Coastal smallholdings*

This stage of the trail follows a tree-shaded catchwater for most of its length, and as such offers seven kilometres of level and easy walking between *H068* and *H083*. Follow the olive-green painted railings – the sound of rushing water will often also guide your way. Sluice gates mark the start of your horizontal trek.

After 20 minutes the path leaves the catchwater to cross a valley by way of a small dam. A brook babbles its way downhill towards Tai Tam Harbour. Then it's back to the catchwater trail. Look out for red-clawed crabs which dart out from under leaves.

As you walk, you circle Obelisk Hill, named for the marker near its peak erected by the Royal Navy at the turn of the 19th century. Separated by exactly one nautical mile, and sitting on the same line of longitude, this and a similar obelisk to the south served as navigational aids.

The path loses its tree cover now and you are treated to glimpses of the harbour, as well as those less appealing radar domes on Mount Parker. Over on the next ridge, made tiny by distance, double-deck buses can be seen trundling their way to Shek O. Suddenly the trees on your right drop away and the village of Lan Nai Wan, with its bright yellow temple (above), is revealed directly beneath. It must be one of the last few places on Hong Kong Island where land is still cultivated.

Hobie cat hideaway: To Tei Wan beach comes to life at weekends

An ebb tide leaves its imprint in the sand

Here you have a choice: keep to the catchwater and the Hong Kong Trail, or descend to Lan Nai Wan and hug the coast. Taking the upper path, you're treated to more open views of Tai Tam Harbour and its weekend population of junks and water skiers. On the other side perch the skin-toned villas of Red Hill, and down on the shore stands that second obelisk. The wide spread of Stanley, from the fort to dragonboat beach, is laid out to the south. Seldom-used paths lead occasionally downhill to the coastal settlements, the few remaining villagers mainly choosing to come and go by boat. The catchwater ends abruptly at *H083*, and a water-eroded track leads you downhill.

The lower route passes through the mostly-ruined villages of Tung Ah, Tung Ah Pui and Ngan Hang. Watch out for doggedly territorial village mutts.

The two paths meet again before descending, by way of a leaf-strewn flight of steps, to the beach at To Tei Wan.

Walking to the far end of the beach, you'll find the Nam Kee Café, which on weekends will provide you with cold drinks, noodles if required, and a shady perch. The dunes are kept from shifting by a fleet of hobiecats dragged up onto the sand. Their owners are ferried over from Stanley on Sundays; at other times, To Tei Wan feels like it could be a hundred miles from the nearest neighbouring settlement.

The steps lead one back uphill, past a wartime pillbox, to Shek O Road. Cross over to catch bus 9 to Shek O, or remain on the near side of the road for buses headed for Central or Shau Kei Wan.

H083 Hobiecat haven at To Tei Wan

Hong Kong Trail

STAGE
8
Tai Long Wan
大浪灣

To Tei Wan 土地灣 >
Tai Long Wan 大浪灣

8.5 km / 2.75 hours

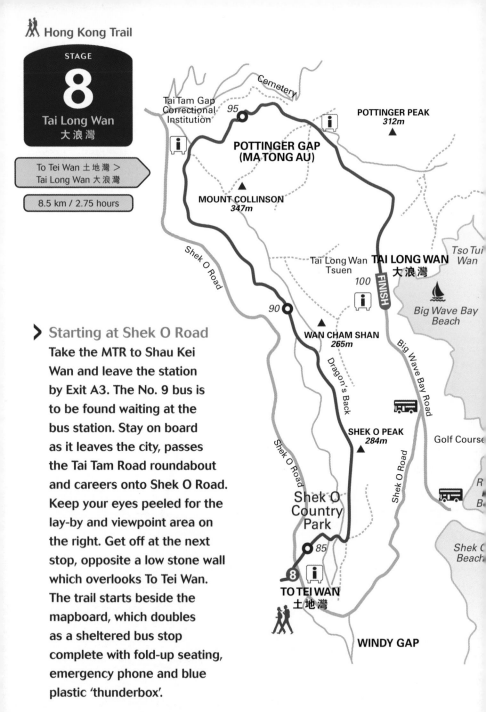

Cemetery

Tai Tam Gap
Correctional
Institution

95

POTTINGER PEAK
312m

POTTINGER GAP
(MA TONG AU)

MOUNT COLLINSON
347m

Shek O Road

Tai Long Wan TAI LONG WAN
Tsuen 大浪灣

Tso Tui
Wan

100

FINISH

Big Wave Bay
Beach

90

WAN CHAM SHAN
265m

Big Wave Bay Road

Dragon's Back

SHEK O PEAK
284m

Golf Course

Shek O Road

Shek O
Country
Park

85

Shek O Road

R
B

Shek O
Beach

> ## Starting at Shek O Road

Take the MTR to Shau Kei
Wan and leave the station
by Exit A3. The No. 9 bus is
to be found waiting at the
bus station. Stay on board
as it leaves the city, passes
the Tai Tam Road roundabout
and careers onto Shek O Road.
Keep your eyes peeled for the
lay-by and viewpoint area on
the right. Get off at the next
stop, opposite a low stone wall
which overlooks To Tei Wan.
The trail starts beside the
mapboard, which doubles
as a sheltered bus stop
complete with fold-up seating,
emergency phone and blue
plastic 'thunderbox'.

8
TO TEI WAN
土地灣

WINDY GAP

Along the Dragon's Back

Beyond the Dragon's Back: The hike's destination Big Wave Bay seen in the distance

H086 Approaching Shek O Peak

Cruise views: Tathong Channe

(If continuing from Stage 7, after a dip in the sea or a stroll along the beach, take a deep breath and then mount the 750 steps up to Shek O Road. *H084* greets you on the 600th step.)

The most demanding segment of the Hong Kong Trail has been saved for last. This section starts off deceptively, under the shade of bamboo and banana trees, but soon changes character to become a stiff climb over a rocky, exposed hillside. Take a rest every now and then to ensure that you'll make it to the top, but also to enjoy the views of Tai Tam Bay that lie behind you.

At the covered pavilion, take the steps on the right up to the Dragon's Back. It's well signposted. The ascent to the ridge is well worth the effort, as you are greeted on arrival by sweeping views of Shek O and the rugged coast below

Into thin air

(following spread). It's a windy spot, popular with weekend paragliders. The trail turns north here and runs a precariously balanced route along the spine of the Dragon's Back, dense shrubbery on either side providing cover for a variety of vocal birds.

The summit of Shek O Peak is crossed, and then a descent is made along an eroded and well-used path. Far below, the villas and swimming pools of Hong Kong's taipans stretch towards the sands of Big Wave Bay. The shouts of beachgoers are somehow lifted by the wind to reach your ears even at this altitude. The auspicious 88th trail marker makes its appearance, and from here on you are treated to some of Hong Kong's best hiking conditions: tunnels of cool foliage, the scent of nature along damp, tree-shaded pathways of gravel, sand, fallen leaves and tree roots – a welcome antidote to the paved sections earlier on.

Vertiginous vantage point

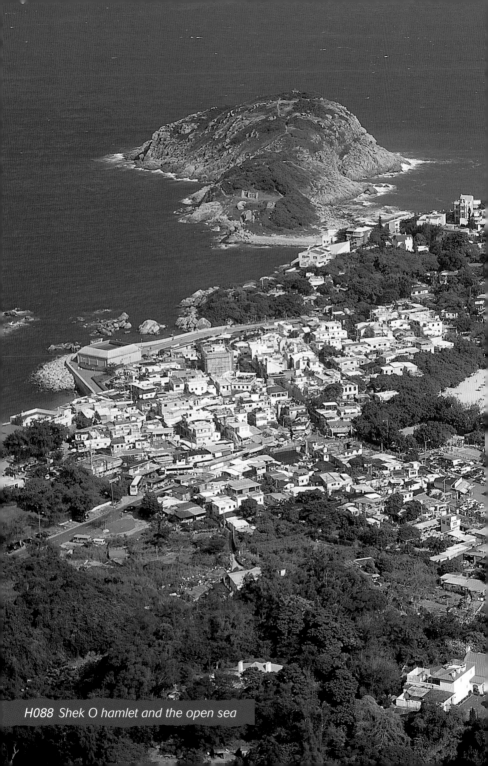

H088 Shek O hamlet and the open sea

Breakers roll in at Big Wave Bay

Seasonal streams cross the winding forest trail, water running between mossy boulders and roots. After some distance, the path joins a cement water services track. Turn right onto the wider road at the end.

Breaks in the greenery allow views of Chai Wan and the impressively regimented terraces of the Chinese hillside cemeteries. At Pottinger Gap, the road ends, seemingly exhausted from pushing its way through such thick undergrowth. Follow the catchment railings, painted in military green, and the Hong Kong Trail hiker's logo appears on a wooden marker pointing the way ahead, down an overgrown flight of steps.

A short descent through damp foliage puts you on the last stretch towards Big Wave Bay. Lights begin to appear in the village below while, behind you, the sun falls towards the ridge of the Dragon's Back. Trail marker *H100* – the very last one – appears just short of the first village house. The sounds of family life and the smells of dinner being prepared reach you from both sides of the trail as you pass between the houses, encountering children playing in the evening sunlight.

Follow the motorable track towards a line of seaside snack shops. The beach, protected on both sides by rocky outcrops, is just a minute's walk away to the left. The village car park is served by buses and minibuses but their schedules are rather erratic. If the timetable (or the villagers) indicate that there are no buses, you will have to walk the short distance to the Shek O Road, where you can pick up the more frequent no. 9 for Shau Kei Wan.

Emergency Help

Of all the dangers naturally present on a Hong Kong hike – snakes, macaques, feral dogs, ravines, flash floods, hill fires, landslides – it's the heat which is most likely to affect you, in the form of sunstroke or dehydration.

It's common to read in the newspapers that a group of teenagers were rescued from a country park by helicopter after feeling slightly ill. But it's important not to abuse the emergency services, for they have wide-ranging responsibilities. The Government Flying Service, for example, provides a 24-hour air ambulance service for those truly in need in remote areas. But it is also responsible for search and rescue operations in the seas around Hong Kong, and it assists the Fire Services Department by water-bombing hill fires.

According to the Hong Kong Police, 54% of emergency calls received in the first half of the year – over half a million of them – were nuisance calls or misdialled. "This could endanger the lives of people at risk by postponing their access to the service," a force spokesman said.

If it is a genuine emergency, you can call for help by way of the public phone lines provided at intervals on remote trails, which put you directly through to the control centres; or on your mobile phone by dialling 999.

Once the call is placed, a chain reaction is set in motion. The control centre informs relevant agencies – such as the Auxiliary Medical Service, the Civil Aviation Department, the Police Force, the Marine Department or the Hospital Authority – and each body will respond to the caller. Make sure your phone is well charged. You'll need to provide your location as accurately as possible, quoting the nearest trail marker or map grid reference or, if at night, shining a torch upon hearing the approach of the rescuers.

It's certainly not to be used as a free ride home after a pleasant day's walking. If nothing else, the chopper will take the hiker either to hospital or to the flying service's base at the airport. Getting home from there could be costlier and more time-consuming than one had planned!

An overland trip along the Silk Road took **Pete Spurrier** from London to China in 1993, and he has lived in Hong Kong since then, exploring the city's backstreets and hiking its hills. When not bribing sampan ladies to transport him to distant islands, he spends his time deciphering the secret language of minibus drivers. Pete's guided walks have appeared in the *South China Morning Post*, in local magazines, and in *The Leisurely and Heritage Hiker's Guide*, also published by FormAsia Books.

Addendum:

Since the first edition of this guidebook was published, we've been delighted to receive questions and feedback from hiking readers. Much of this has helped us update the guide each time. One query stands out: What to do if you're an overseas visitor to Hong Kong, with perhaps a day or two spare to tread the trails after a business trip or family visit? You are unlikely to know where the free country park campsites are located, or where to buy walking gear, stove gas and other outdoors necessities. With this in mind, we list the following websites as sources of useful information.

Outdoor Specialists:
http://www.chamonix.com.hk/shop.html
http://www.alink.com.hk/
http://www.protrek.com.hk/index.php?lang=en

HKSAR recommended campsites:
http://www.afcd.gov.hk/english/country/cou_vis/cou_vis_cam/cou_vis_cam_cam/cou_vis_cam_cam.html

The Serious Hiker's Guide to Hong Kong

Published by:
FormAsia Books Limited
706 Yu Yuet Lai Building
45 Wyndham Street
Central, Hong Kong
www.formasiabooks.com

Ninth Edition Published 2014
ISBN 978-988-98269-2-5

Text and photographs
©FormAsia Books Limited

Written by Pete Spurrier
Photography by Kwan Kwong Chung/
Sathish Gobinath

Produced by Format Limited, Hong Kong
 Design: Alice Yim/Maggie Wan
 Digital production: Nelson Pun/
 Dickson Chou/Fred Yuen
 Maps: Dickson Chou/Edwin Chiu/
 Sunny Chan
 Production supervision: Jenny Choi

Printed in Hong Kong by
Treasure Printing Company Limited
Images scanned by
Sky Art Graphic Company Limited, Hong Kong